Volcano Earthquake Mazes

Roger Moreau

Sterling Publishing Co., Inc.
New York

10 9 8 7 6 5 4 3 2 1

Published by Sterling Publishing Company, Inc.
387 Park Avenue South, New York, N.Y. 10016
© 2000 by Roger Moreau
Distributed in Canada by Sterling Publishing
℅ Canadian Manda Group, One Atlantic Avenue, Suite 105
Toronto, Ontario, Canada M6K 3E7
Distributed in Great Britain and Europe by Chris Lloyd
463 Ashley Road, Parkstone, Poole, Dorset, BH14 0AX, England
Distributed in Australia by Capricorn Link (Australia) Pty Ltd.
P.O. Box 6651, Baulkham Hills, Business Centre, NSW 2153, Australia
Manufactured in the United States of America

Sterling ISBN 0-8069-7121-5

Contents

A Note on the Suggested Use of This Book...4
Introduction...5
Volcanoes...6
Volcano Types...7

Mazes
Mount Vesuvius...8
Mount Pelée...10
Hawaii's Lava Tubes...12
Keep an Eye on Mount St. Helens...14
The Warning...16
There She Blows!...17
Lava Everywhere...18
This Doesn't Look Good...20
The Calm Before the Eruption?...22
It Could Go Anytime!...24
Earthquakes...25
Leave the Building...26
Get Off the Bridge...27
Shake, Rattle, and Roll...28
Shut Off the Gas...30
Demolished...32
Earthquake Detection...34
The Alaska Quake...36
Help!...37
Tsunami...38
The Ruins...40

Congratulations/Cover Solution...42
Maze Guides...43
Index...64

A Note on the Suggested Use of This Book

As you work your way through the pages of this book, try not to mark them. This will enable you to take this journey over and over again and will give your friends a chance to take the same journey that you took with all of the same dangers that you had to face.

Special Warning: When the way looks too difficult, avoid the temptation to start at the end and work your way backwards. This technique would be a violation of the rules.

Cover Maze: While you were observing the tranquil interior of this inactive volcano, it decided to erupt. Without warning! The earthquake that accompanies it isn't helping either. Oh, if you could just be one of those birds and fly away. Sorry! You've got no time to waste. Find a clear path down the mountain, avoid the avalanching boulders, and get to the kayak on the river.

INTRODUCTION

The Earth is not a solid, hard rock as it appears. In fact, it is only the thin crust of the surface that is rigid and hard. Beneath is a churning mass kept in a fluid state by pressure and heat. The hard crust of the surface makes up the continents and seafloors that provide the earth we are familiar with. Underneath, as the fluid material, called the mantle, moves upward, cools, and sinks, it causes the crust to crack. These cracks, or rifts, create areas called plates, of which there are about 20. As these plates slowly move, volcanic and earthquake activity at the rifts occur and are often interrelated. This interaction of the plates is known as plate tectonics.

The great power and force that volcanic and earthquake activity can bring are very destructive and beyond man's ability to prevent or control. If scientists could predict and warn of a volcanic eruption and/or an earthquake, this destruction could be prevented and many lives saved. So far, they have had some success predicting volcanic eruptions, but earthquakes go virtually undetected. Still, the effort is ongoing. Periodically, progress is made. Damage can be minimized with tough earthquake-resistant building codes. Structures that would have collapsed in the past are built in ways that enable them to move when the earth shakes. The development of new instruments has helped us to understand earth movement, and hopefully the day will come when a coming quake can be predicted in enough time to save lives.

You can help the efforts to understand these two natural forces by observing them when they occur. This is your mission as you journey forth on the following pages. Many times you will be at the edge of a volcano the moment it erupts or be in the area when an earthquake hits and you'll have only minutes to escape. Your experiences will be intense. Have courage. Use good judgment and don't give up. Good luck!

Volcanoes

A volcano is an opening where hot molten rock in liquid form, known as magma, spews up from the interior of the Earth onto the Earth's surface. Most of the time the magma will create a mountain as its layers cool one on top of another. This process can happen quickly or over a long period of time. If the magma forms underwater, the resulting "pile" will result in an island if it rises to the surface.

There are basically two ways that magma comes to the surface: explosive and quiet. When it is explosive, an entire mountain or island can disappear. When it is quiet, a land mass grows.

There are about 550 known volcanoes. Some have become well known because of the death and destruction they have caused. For example, when Vesuvius erupted in A.D. 79, 16,000 died. Tambora killed 92,000 in 1815; Krakatau 36,000 in 1883.

Some volcanoes erupt on a regular basis. Others are intermittent, erupting periodically when the heat has built up. Then there are the dormant volcanoes. They have been quiet for a long period, but there is always the possibility that they will become active. Finally, there are the extinct volcanoes that will probably never erupt again.

Most volcanoes can be found within an area known as the Pacific "Ring of Fire," which seems to be located along the rifts in the plates of the Earth's crust. This is because as the active plates come in contact with each other, heat builds up, creating magma. The magma oozes up through the rifts and onto the crust, causing volcanic eruptions. The Pacific Ring of Fire is composed of many volcanic islands and coastal volcanoes along the western side of the North and South American continents.

Pacific Ring of Fire

Each dot indicates volcanic activity.

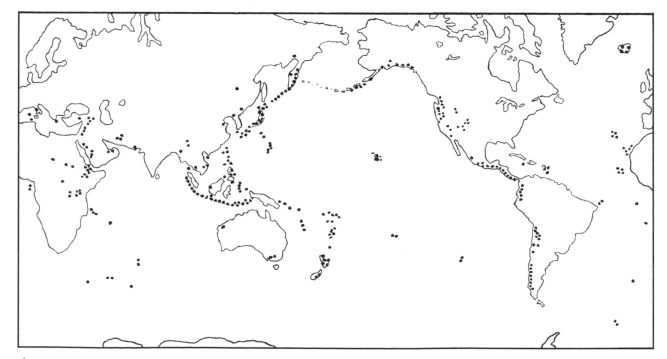

Volcano Types

Follow the path from each volcano type and place the number in the box that will identify it by name.

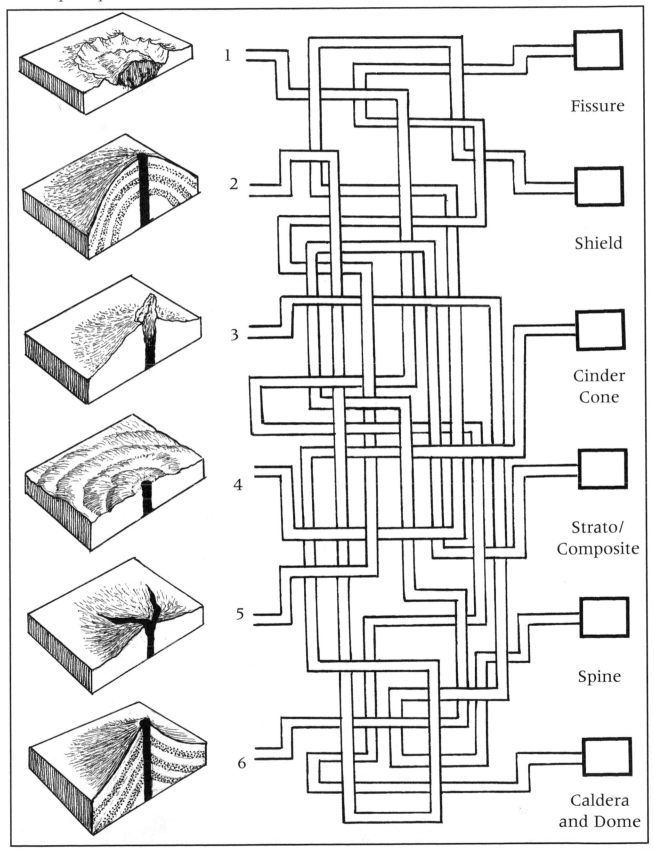

Fissure

Shield

Cinder Cone

Strato/ Composite

Spine

Caldera and Dome

Mount Vesuvius

It is one o'clock in the afternoon, August 24, A.D. 79. Vesuvius is blasting forth with an eruption that will bury the city of Pompeii. Find a clear path through Pompeii and escape in the boat at the pier.

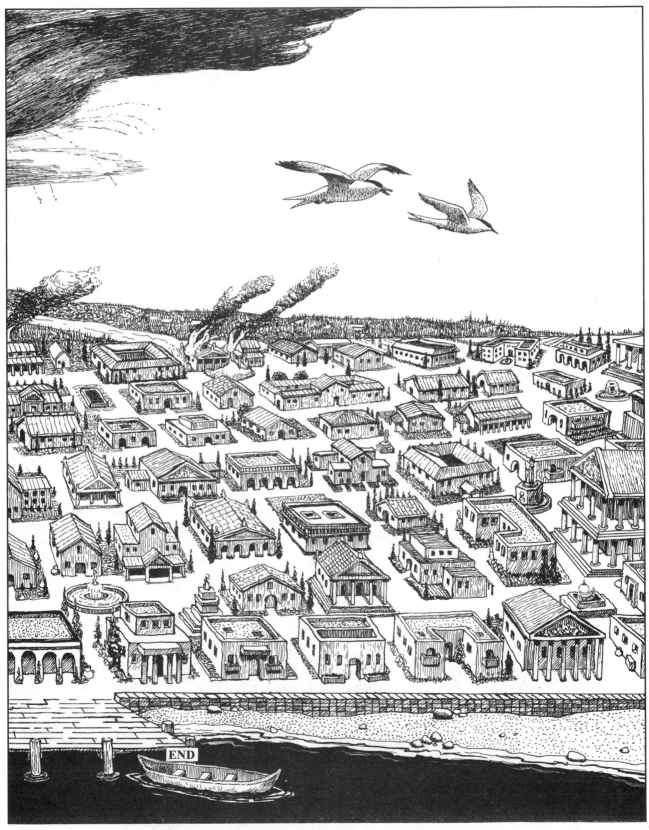

9

Mount Pelée

This eruption destroyed the port of St. Pierre on Martinique in 1902. Close obser-

vation shows that this is a spine volcano. Now that you've discovered this fact, descend in a hurry by finding a clear path to the bottom right corner.

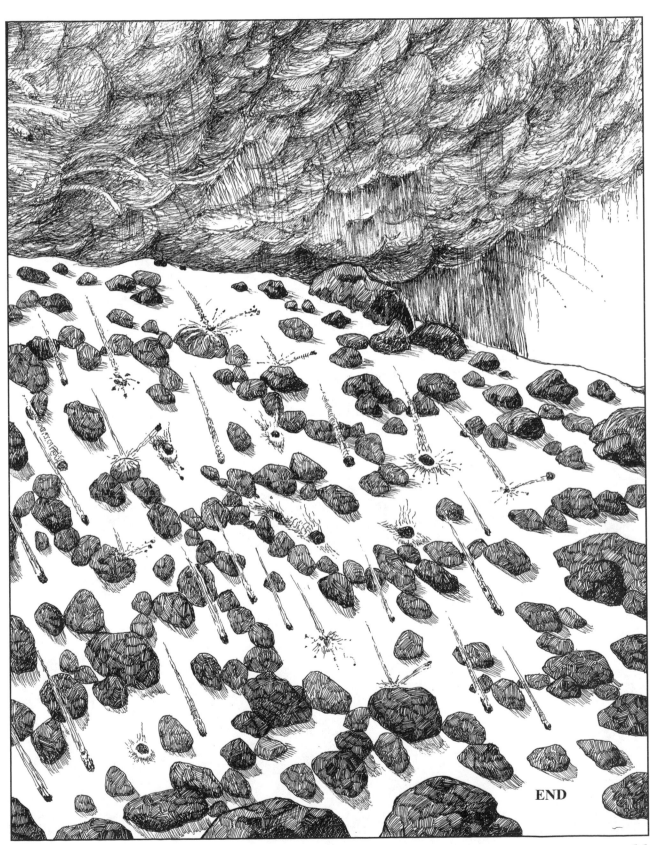

END

Hawaii's Lava Tubes

Lava tubes form when the outer surface of a lava flow hardens with contact to air.

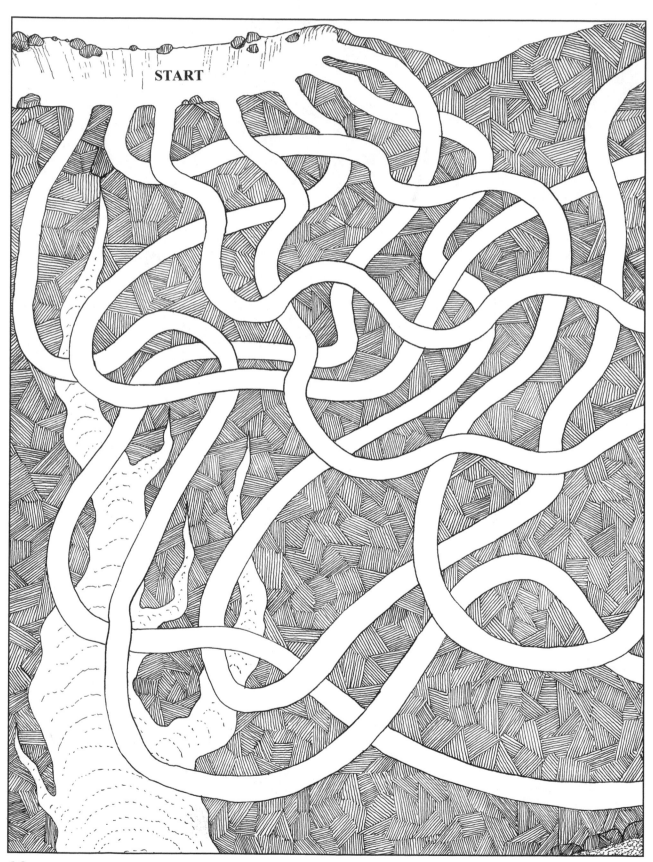

START

The inner lava keeps flowing, leaving a hollow tunnel. Find your way to the ocean's edge through the tunnel that will get you there.

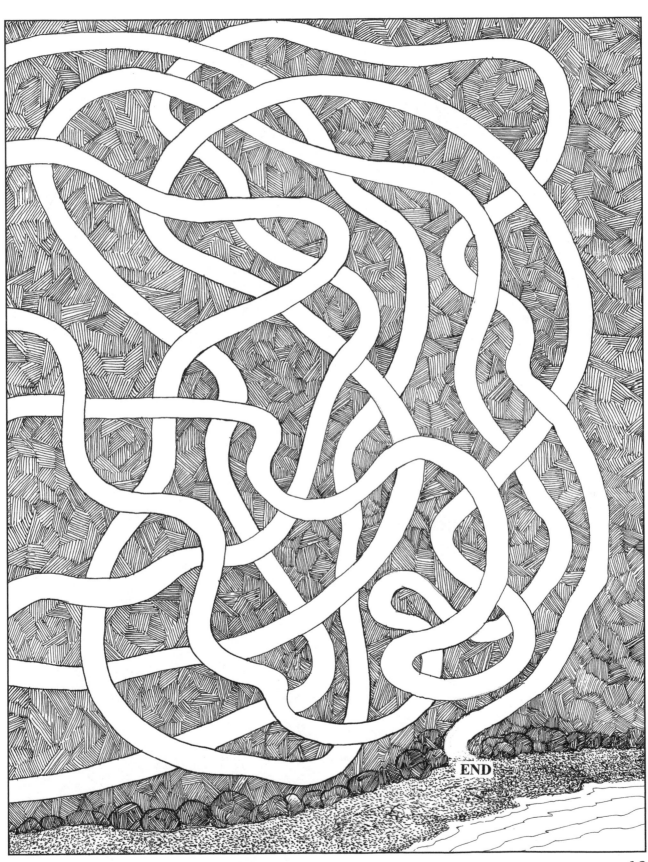

Keep an Eye on Mount St. Helens

These sensors will monitor what's going on deep inside the volcano. Check each monitor for a reading by visiting each one only once-and do not backtrack.

The Warning

That little puff of smoke is a warning that this volcano could erupt. Find a lava tube that will enable you to put down two probes-one on each side of the volcano.

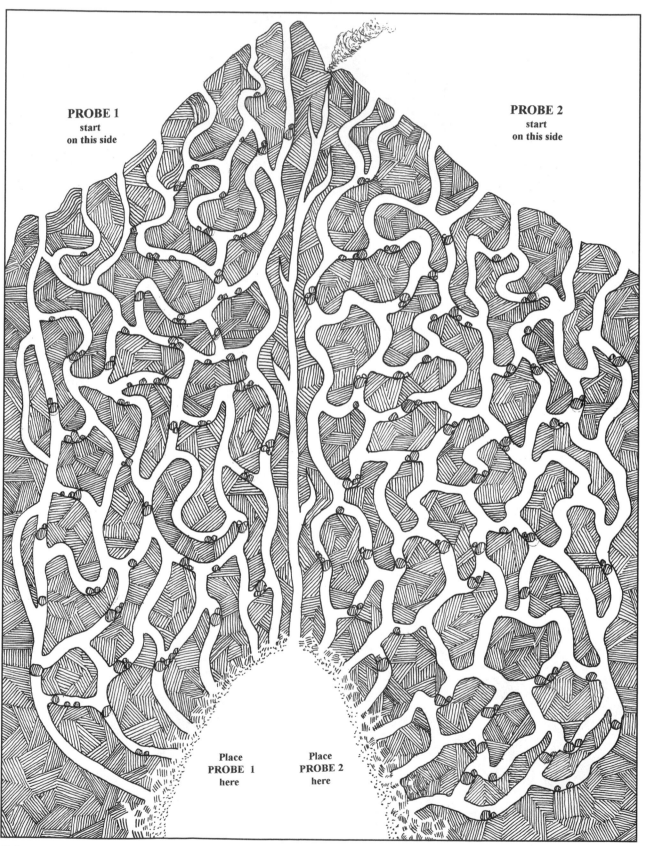

There She Blows!

She's erupted before you've had a chance to get out. With your special suit that will resist the blast on, you can still get out if you hurry.

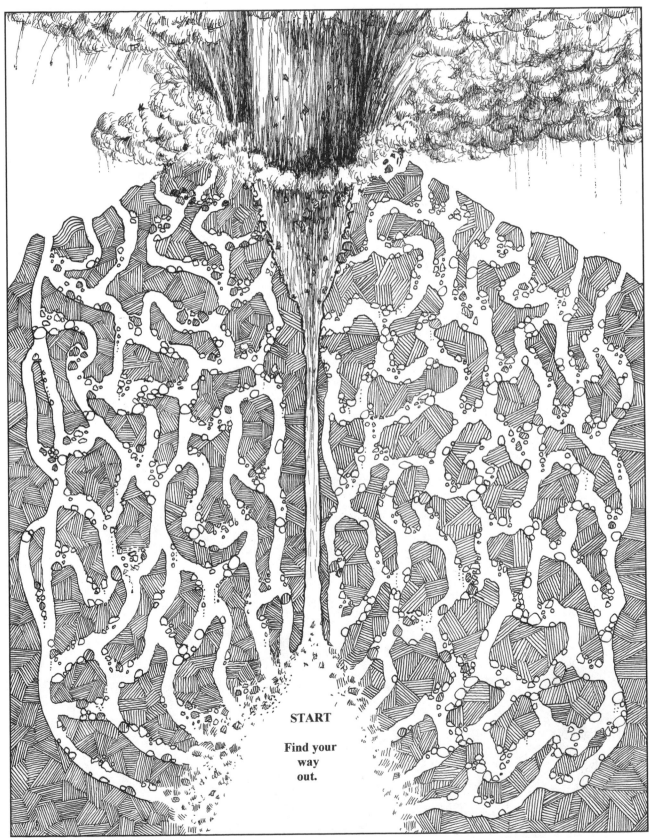

START

Find your way out.

Lava Everywhere

You'd better get to the helicopter before it's too late.

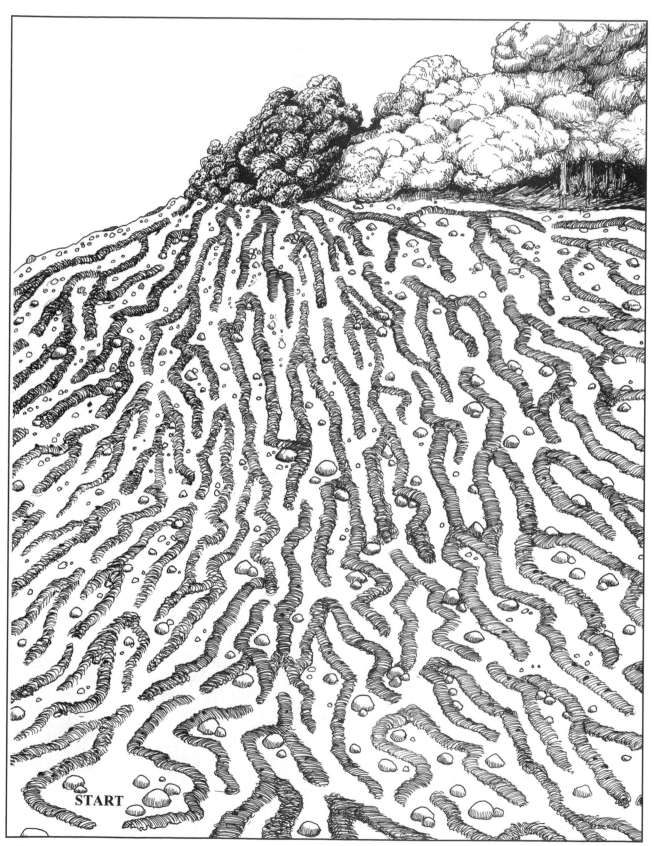

START

This Doesn't Look Good

Mexico has many volcanoes. Towns are sometimes very close to these volcanoes.

START

It looks like something big is about to happen, so get out of town fast by finding a clear path.

ESCAPE →

The Calm before the Eruption?

Observe this crater and then find a clear path to the waiting sports utility vehicle.

START

END

23

It Could Go Anytime!

Get down as fast as you can!

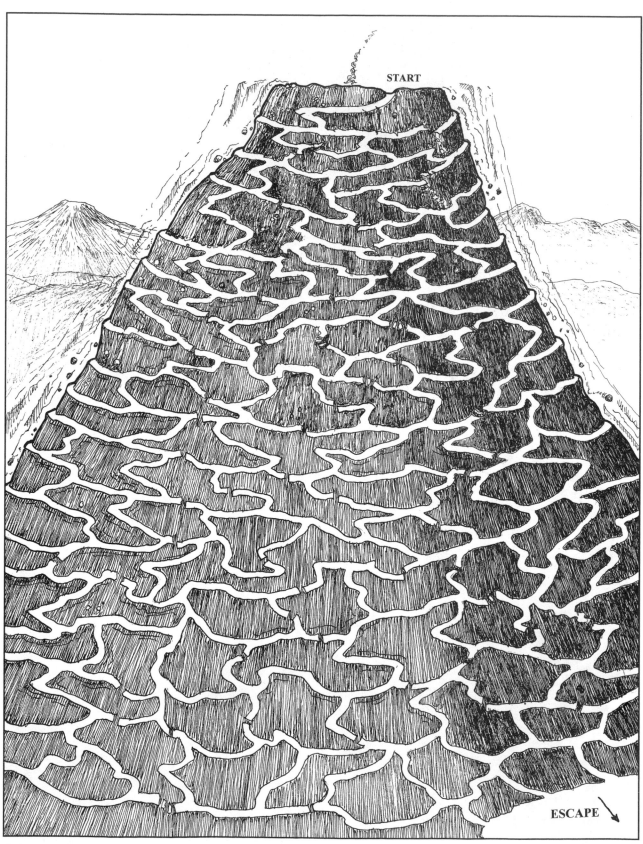

Earthquakes

When a piece of the earth moves, it is called an earthquake. Earthquakes originate in fractures called faults. Many faults occur where the plates of the earth butt against each other. The Pacific Ring of Fire, for example, is a very active earthquake area. As stresses develop along a fault line and pressure builds until the crust can no longer hold, the crust gives way and an earthquake occurs.

Earthquakes have caused great damage and taken many lives over the years. In 1985, Mexico and Columbia were struck by two earthquakes only two months apart, killing more than 32,000 people. When the ground shifted on April 18, 1906, along the San Andreas fault under the city of San Francisco, many lives were lost and most of the city was demolished. Sometimes a tidal wave, called a tsunami, accompanies quakes that are in and around the oceans. As the tsunami slams into the shoreline, additional destruction occurs, such as in Hilo, Hawaii, in 1946 and Anchorage, Alaska, in 1964.

Scientists have developed a scale to indicate the severity of earthquakes and invented instruments to measure them. There are two scales: the Mercalli and the Richter. The Richter scale is the one that most people are familiar with, and a commonly used instrument is a seismometer.

Earthquake Faults   **The Richter Scale**

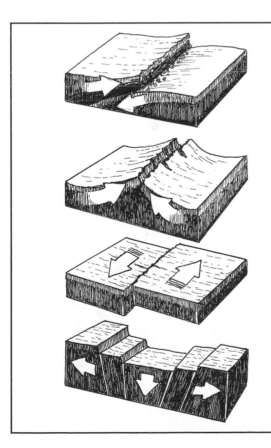

Subduction
One plate goes under a second plate.

Thrust
Plates hit head-on.

Strike-Slip
Horizontal motion.

Down-Dropped
When plates move away from each other.

2.5 Generally not felt, but recorded on seismometers.
3.5 Felt by many people.
4.5 Some local damage might occur.
6.0 A destructive earthquake.
7.0 A major earthquake.
8.0 and up Great earthquake

Leave the Building

Get out of this building by descending the sheets, climbing over the junk, and climbing out if necessary, but do not jump across the openings.

Get Off the Bridge

The cables holding the Golden Gate Bridge are breaking. This traffic jam has stopped all cars, so get out and run for it.

Shake, Rattle, and Roll

The earthquake is breaking up this freeway in a bad way. See if you can find your way off before it's too late.

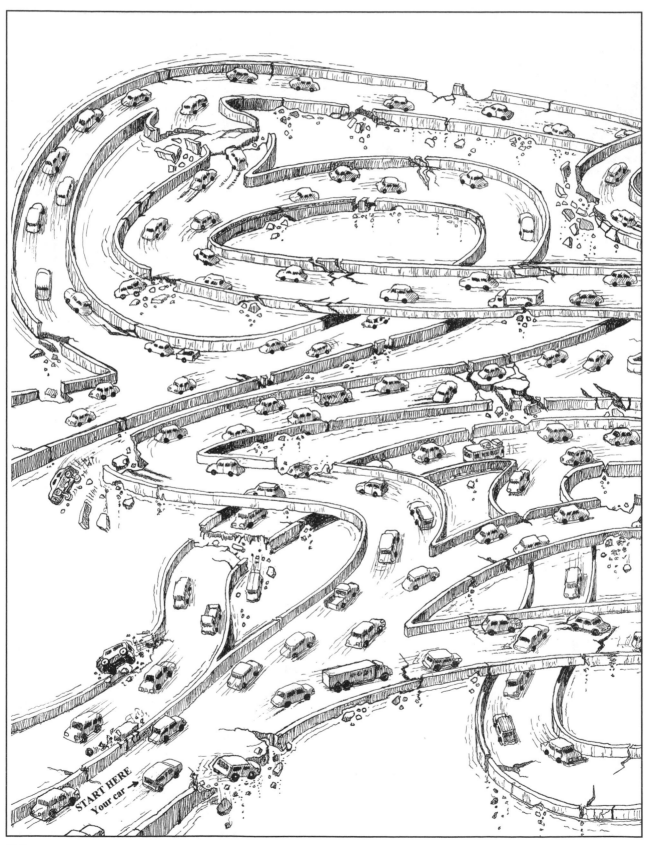

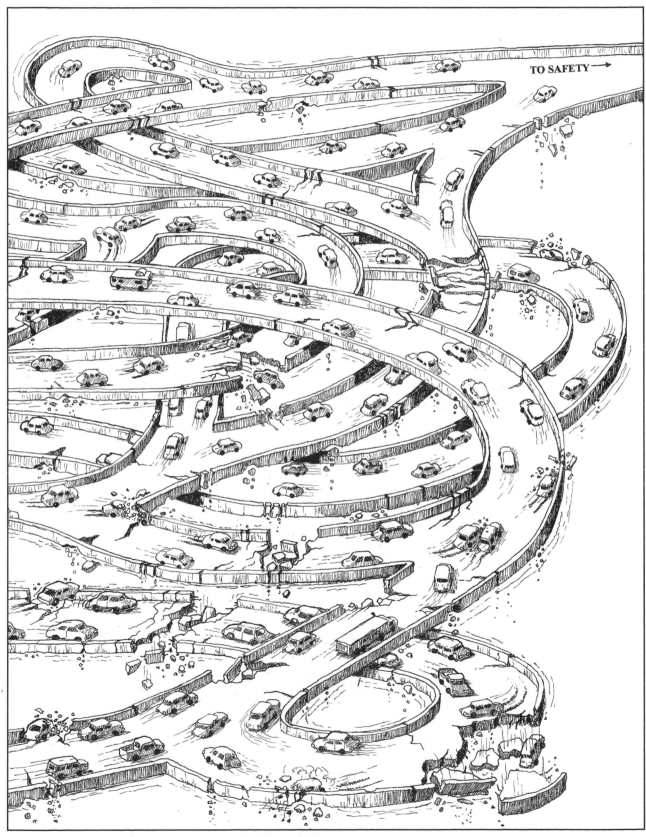

TO SAFETY →

Shut Off the Gas

One of the biggest dangers when an earthquake hits is broken gas lines. To turn

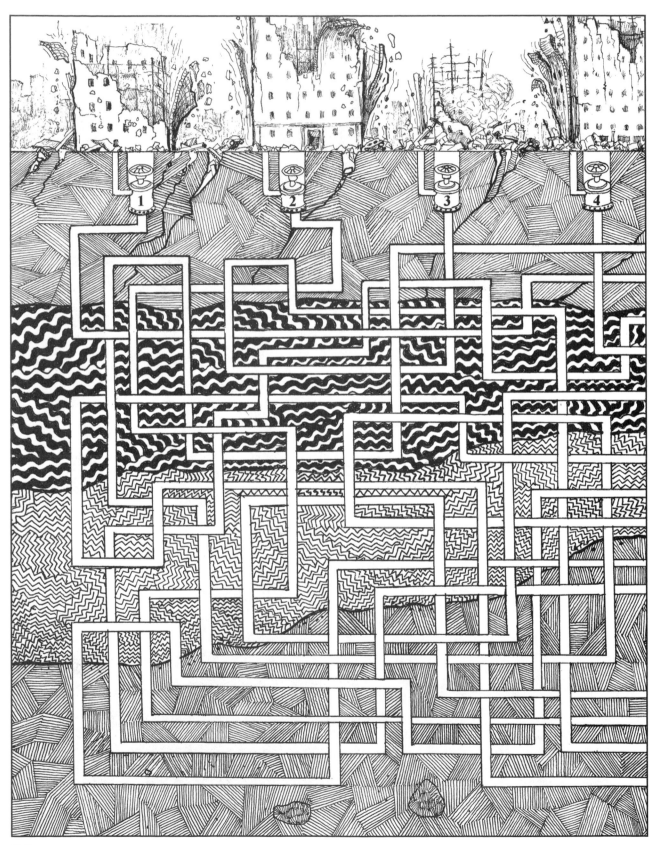

these gas lines off, you must do it in order one through seven. To do this, begin on the right and follow each line. Place the valve number on the unnumbered valve.

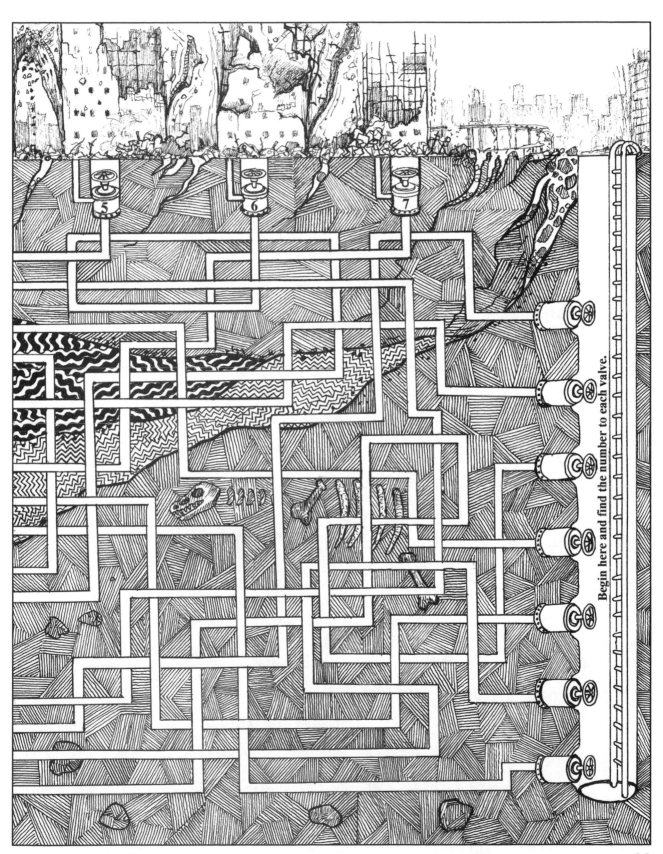

Begin here and find the number to each valve.

Demolished

The 1906 San Francisco earthquake demolished the city. It has happened again! Find a clear road across the city and escape.

Earthquake Detection

There are many scientific instruments to monitor and measure earthquakes. The

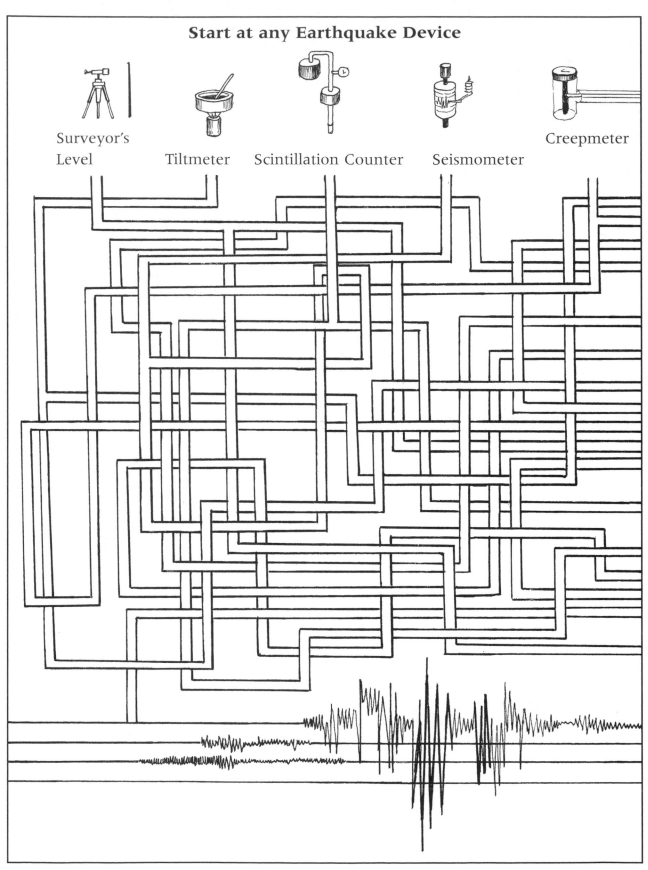

Start at any Earthquake Device

Surveyor's Level

Tiltmeter

Scintillation Counter

Seismometer

Creepmeter

force of the San Francisco quake is indicated by the very jagged line below. Find out which instrument monitored the quake by following the instrument's connection to the line.

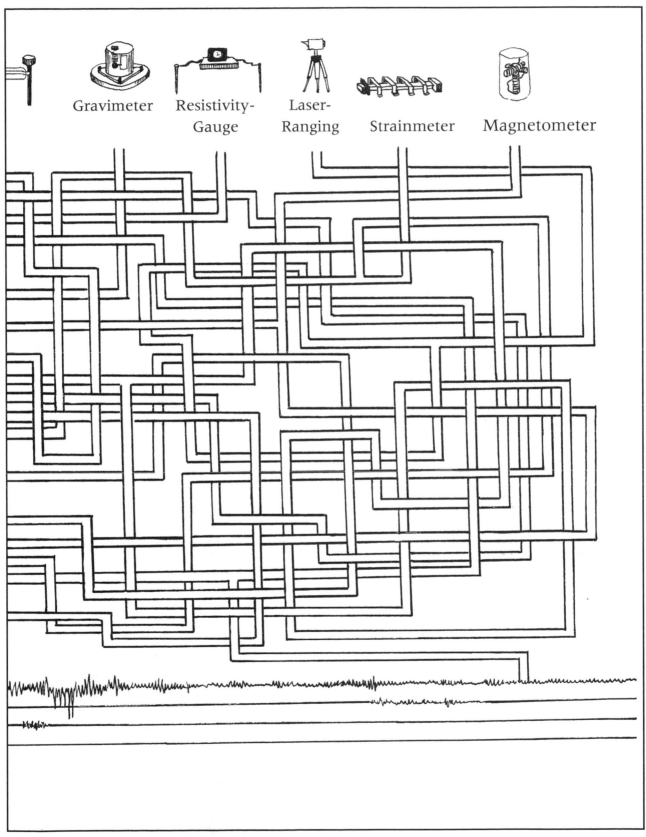

The Alaska Quake

On March 28, 1964, an 8.6 earthquake hit Anchorage, Alaska. It was devastating. See if anyone is injured in that car by finding a clear path to it.

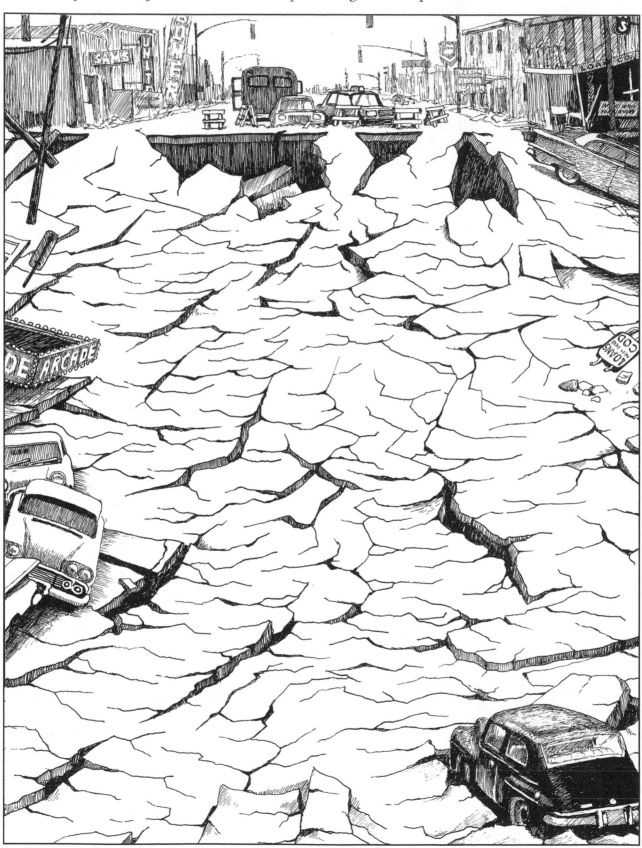

Help!

Help the family in this house find their way to the road by moving from ice block to connecting ice block.

Tsunami

A tsunami is a giant wave, or a tidal wave, that is caused by an earthquake. The

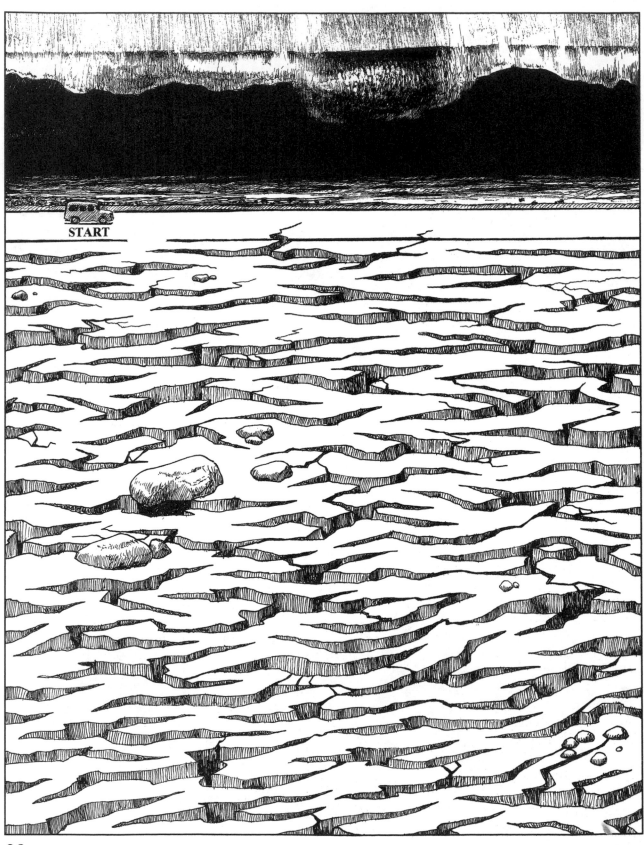

START

Alaska quake produced a tsunami that caused a lot of damage. Escape from this tsunami by cutting across the field ahead of the wave. Avoid the cracks.

SAFETY

The Ruins

Mexico suffers many earthquakes. Here lies the ruins of a small town as a result.

Make your way through the remains of the town to the church. Find a clear path, and hopefully the town's people will be there.

Congratulations

You have experienced and survived the two most violent natural forces that can occur on Earth: volcanic eruptions and earthquakes. Hopefully, you have learned from your experiences. You've had to be "quick" to escape falling ash, boulders, flowing magma, and explosions. You've fled crumbling buildings, falling bridges, and freeways. But just as important, you've helped in saving lives, worked with science, and increased your knowledge about what causes these events. Gaining greater knowledge about any topic will always make you a better person, as it has in this case.

Maze Guides

If you have any trouble finding your way through the mazes in this book, use the guides on the following pages. These guides should be used only in the case of an emergency. The guide shown below is for the cover maze.

Volcano Types

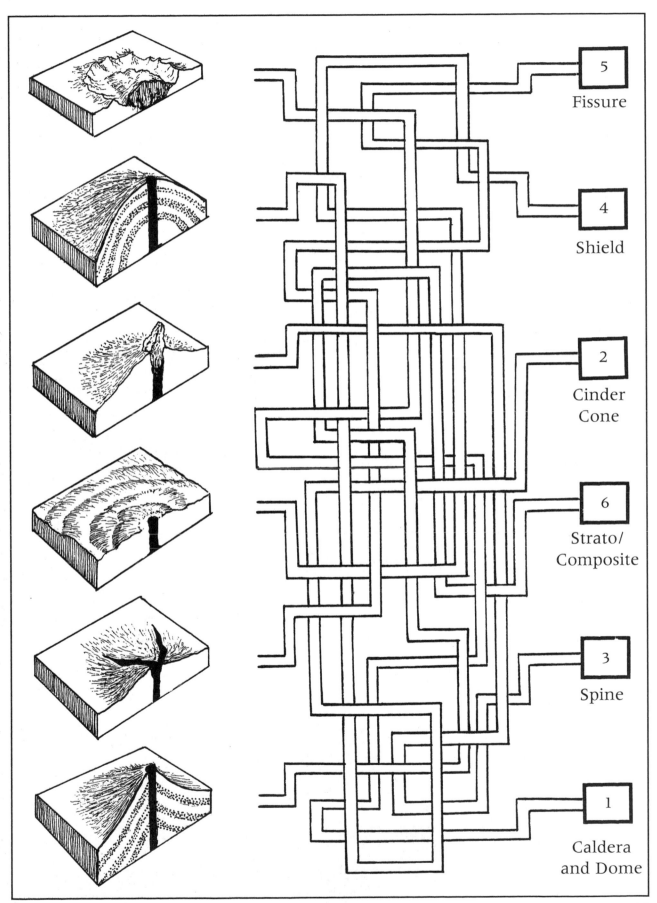

5   Fissure

4   Shield

2   Cinder Cone

6   Strato/ Composite

3   Spine

1   Caldera and Dome

START

END

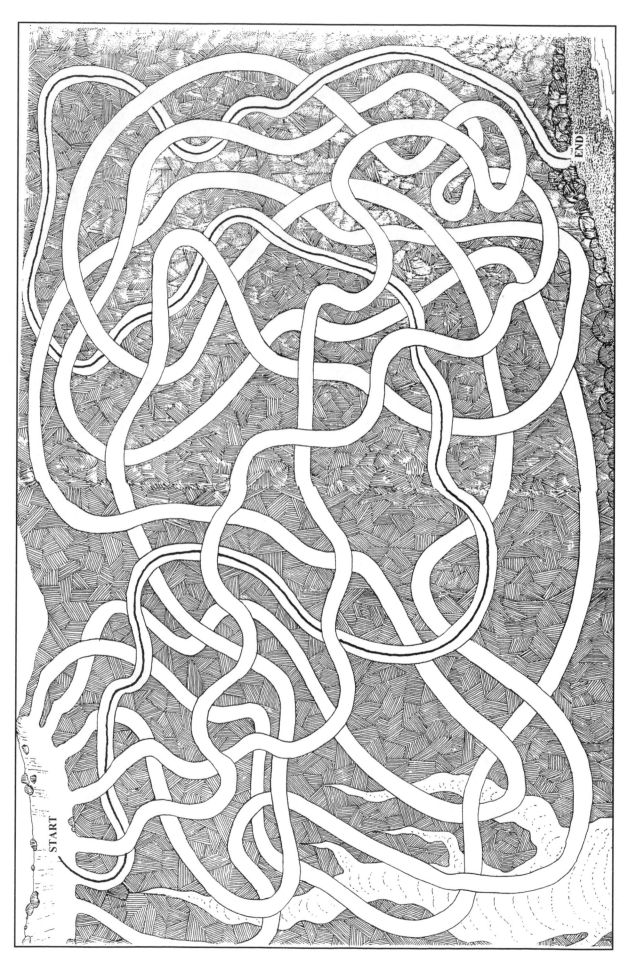

START

END

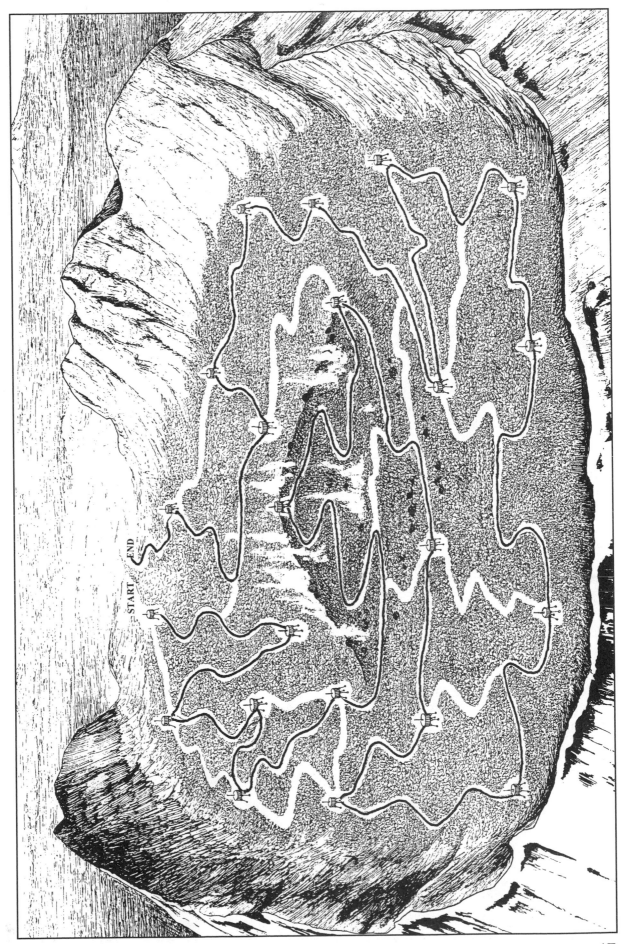

The Warning

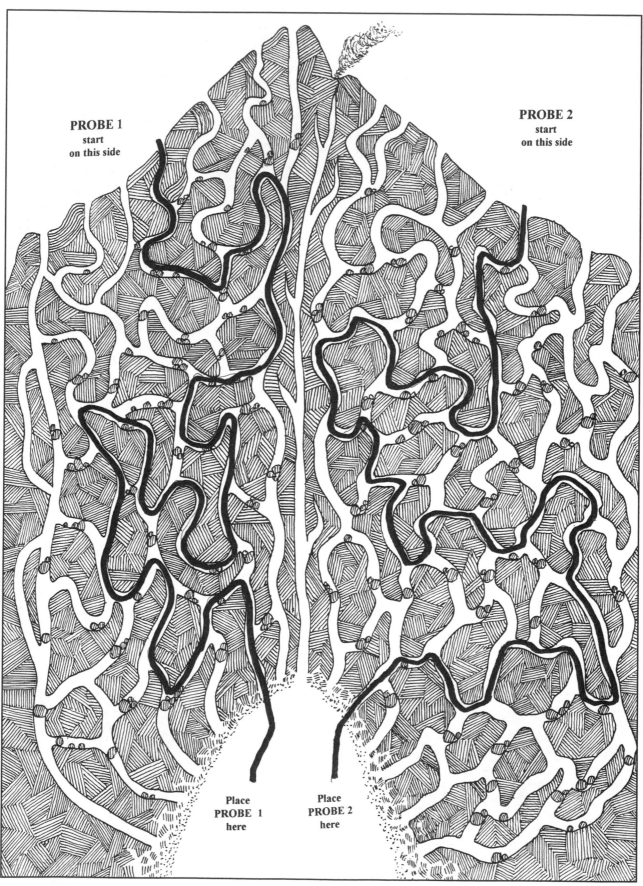

There She Blows!

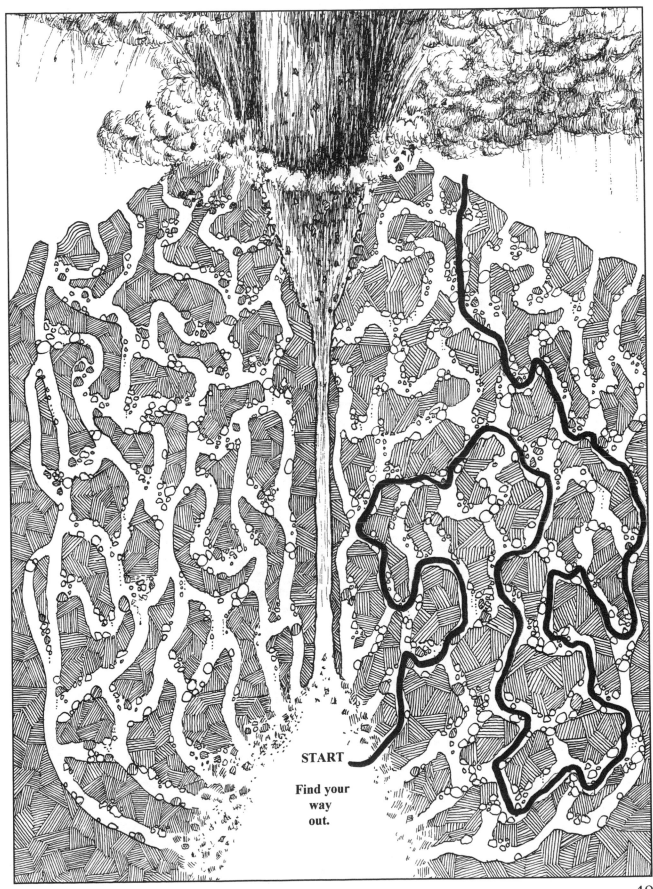

START

Find your way out.

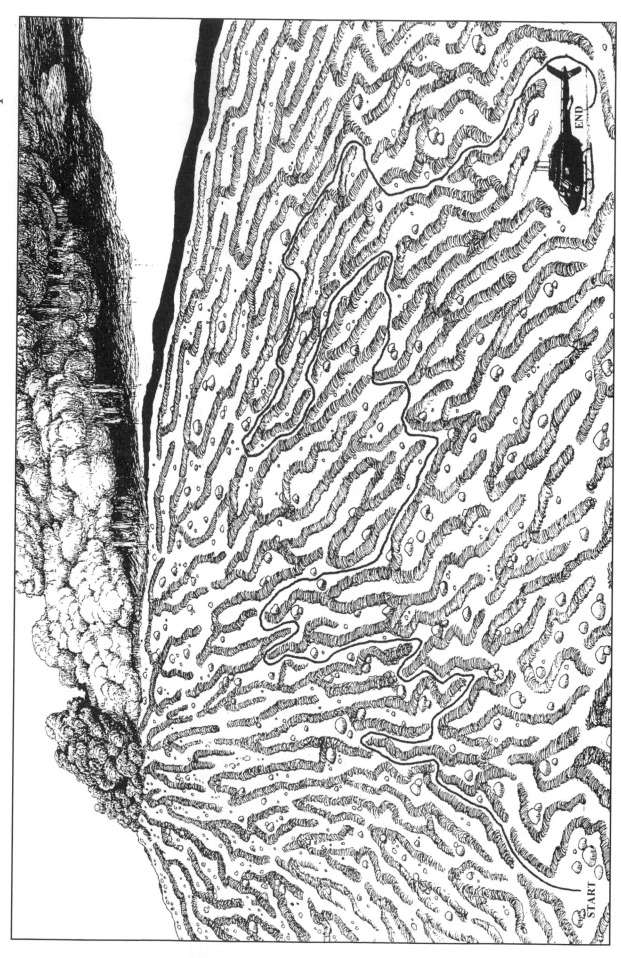

51

The Calm Before the Eruption?

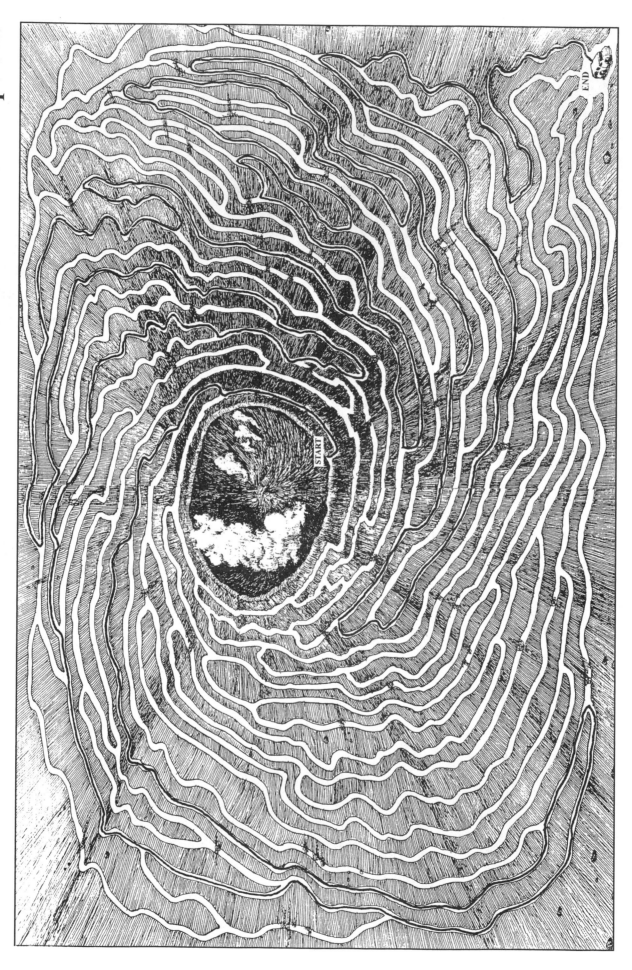

START

END

It Could Go Anytime!

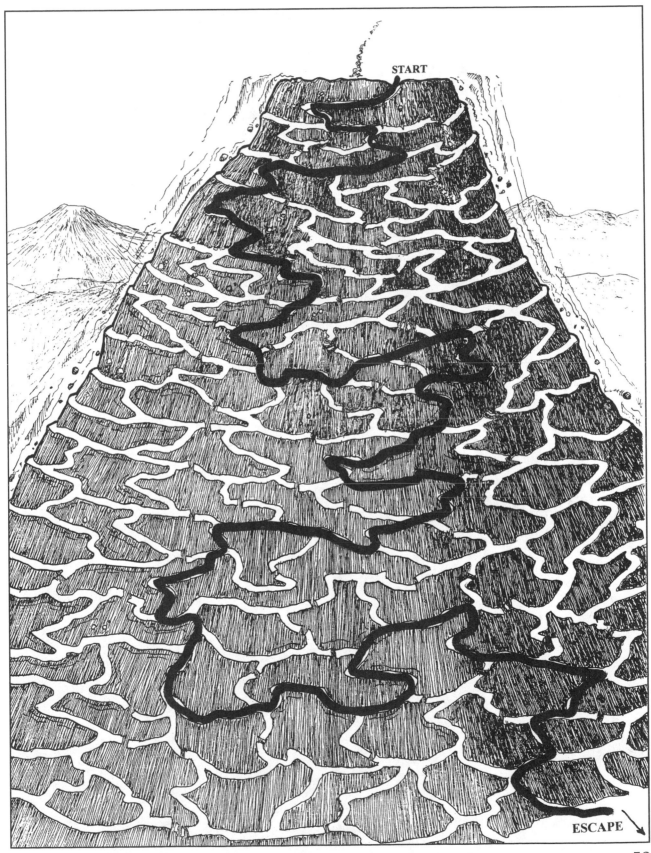

Leave the Building

Get Off the Bridge

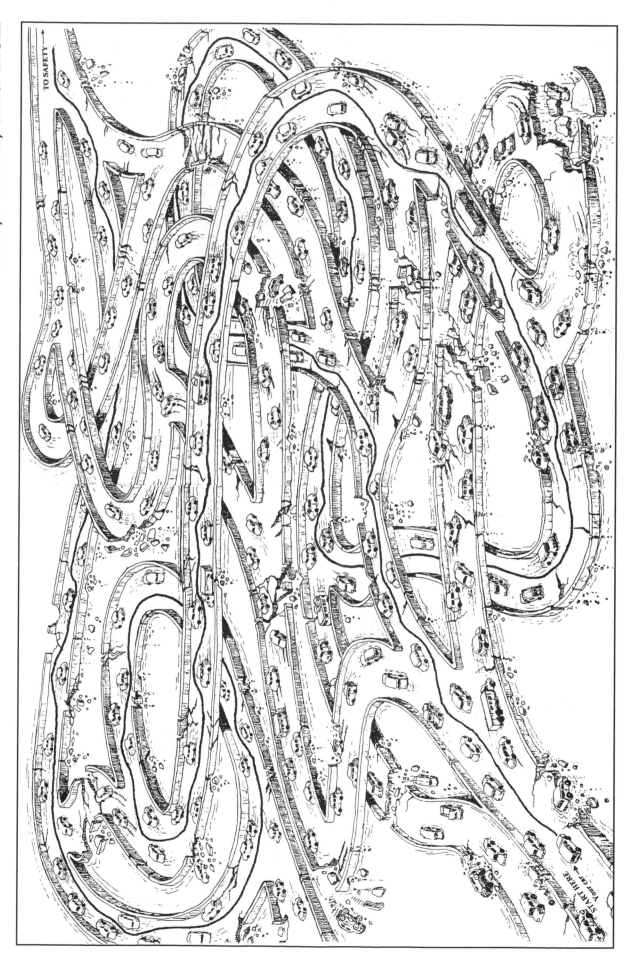

Shut Off the Gas

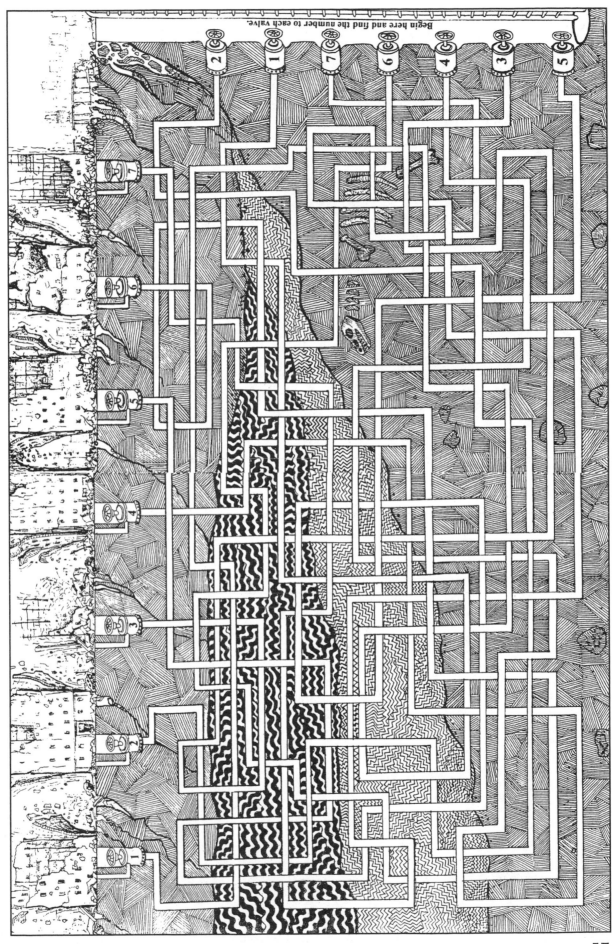

Begin here and find the number to each valve.

Earthquake Detection

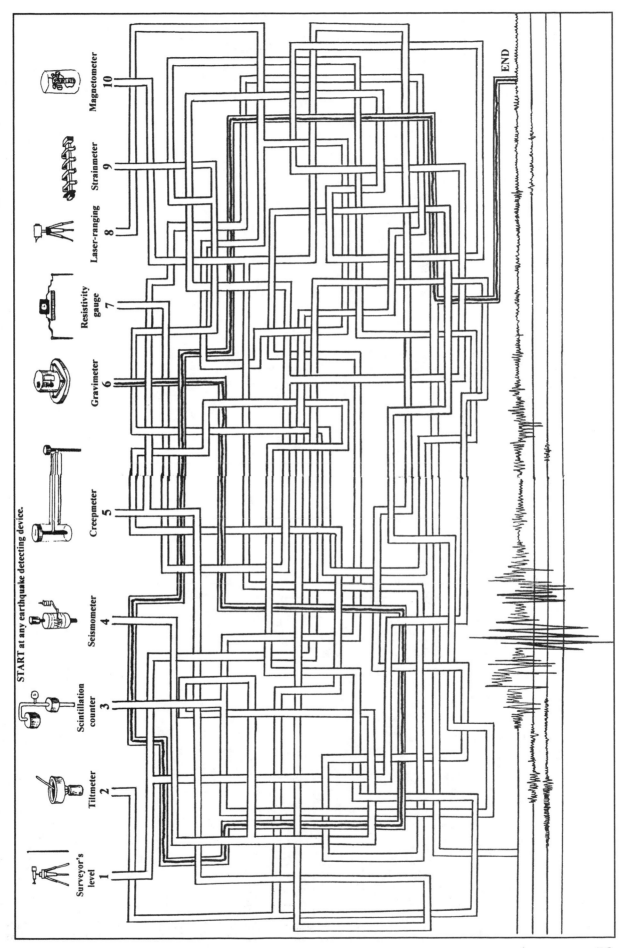

START at any earthquake detecting device.

Surveyor's level 1
Tiltmeter 2
Scintillation counter 3
Seismometer 4
Creepmeter 5
Gravimeter 6
Resistivity gauge 7
Laser-ranging 8
Strainmeter 9
Magnetometer 10

END

The Alaska Quake

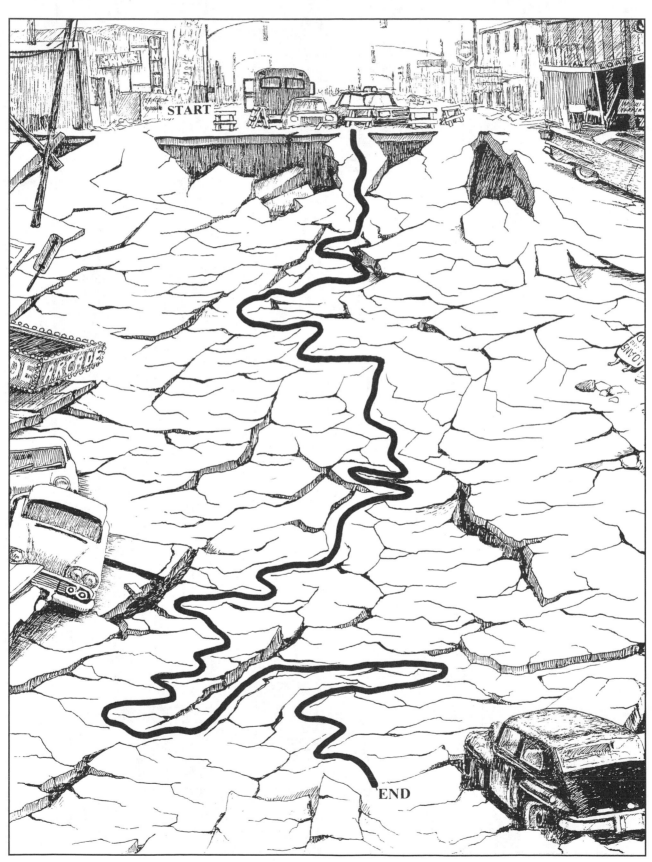

Help!

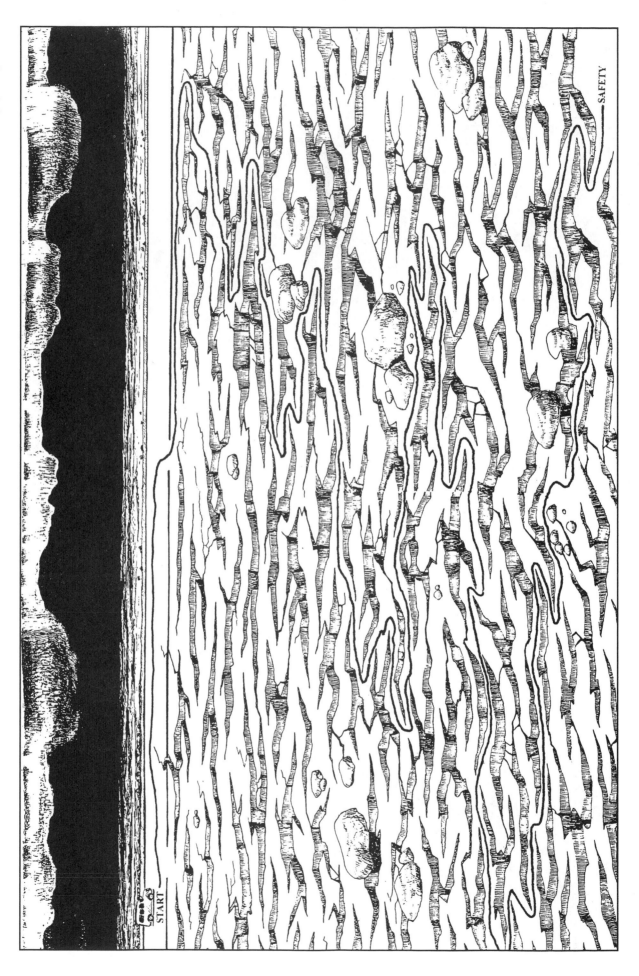

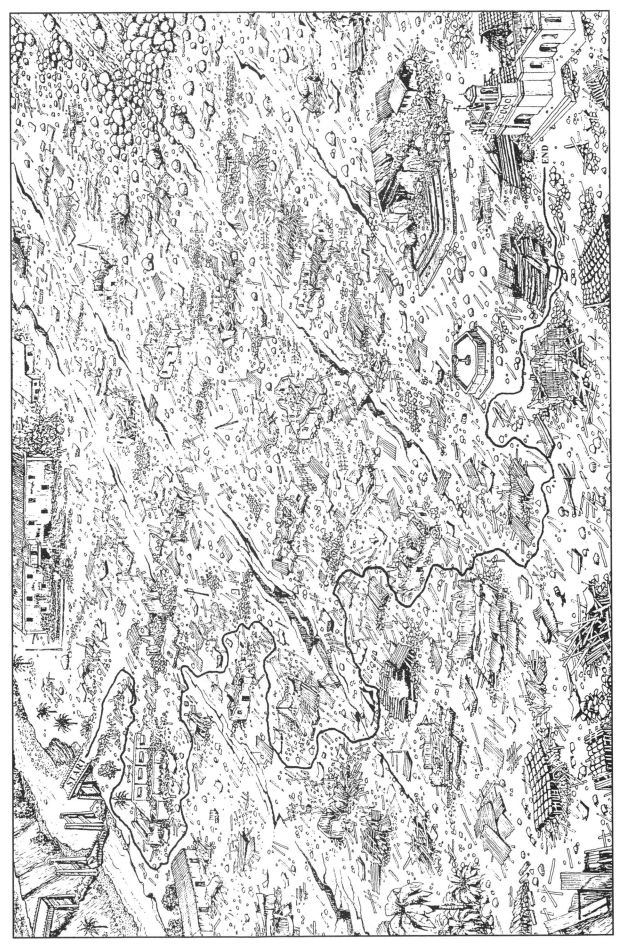

Index

Alaska quake, 25, 36-37, 60, 61
Caldera and dome volcanoe, 7, 43
Cinder cone volcano, 7, 43
Crater, 22
Creepmeter, 34-35, 59
Down-dropped fault, 25
Earthquakes
    Alaska, 25, 36-39
    Columbia, 25
    description of, 25
    detection, 34-35, 59
    Mexico, 25, 40-41, 63
    San Francisco, 25, 27, 32-35
Faults, 25
Fissure volcano, 7, 43
Golden Gate Bridge, 27, 55
Grayimeter, 34-35, 59
Hawaii's lava tubes, 12-13, 46
Krakatau, 6
Laser-ranging monitor, 34-35, 59
Lava, 18-19, 8
Lava tubes, 12-13, 16-17, 46, 47
Magma, 6
Magnetometer, 34-35, 59
Martinique, 10
Mercalli Scale, 25
Mexico
    earthquake, 40-41, 63
    volcano, 20-21, 51
Pacific Ring of Fire, 6, 25
Pelée, 10-11, 45

Pile, 6
Pompeii, 8-9, 44
Resistivity gauge, 34-35, 59
Richter Scale, 25
San Andreas fault, 25
Scintillation counter, 34-35, 59
Seismometer, 25, 34-35, 59
Spine earthquake, 7, 10-11, 43
St. Helens, 14-15, 47
St. Pierre, 10, 45
Strainmeter, 34-35, 59
Strato/composite earthquake, 7, 43
Strike-slip fault, 25
Subduction fault, 25
San Francisco earthquake, 25, 32-33,
Surveyor's level, 34-35, 59
Tambora, 6
Thrust fault, 25
Tidal wave, 24, 38-39, 62
Tiltmeter, 34-35, 59
Tsunami, 25, 38-39, 62
Vesuvius, 6, 8-9, 44
Volcanoes
    description of, 6
    Krakatau, 6
    Pelée, 10-11, 45
    Tambora, 6
    types of, 7, 43
    Vesuvius, 6, 8-9, 44